Lerner **SPORTS**

ALL–STAR
SMACK‹‹‹
››DOWN

JOE BURROW VS. DAN MARINO

WHO WOULD WIN?

JIM GIGLIOTTI

Lerner Publications ◆ Minneapolis

SPORTS THRILLS MEET RESEARCH SKILLS

Lerner SPORTS

Free Database Trial: **lernersports.com**

Lerner Publications Company
An imprint of Lerner Publishing Group, Inc.
241 First Avenue North
Minneapolis, MN 55401 USA

For reading levels and more information, look up this title at www.lernerbooks.com.

Main body text set in Aptifer Sans LT Pro.
Typeface provided by Linotype AG.

Library of Congress Cataloging-in-Publication Data

Names: Gigliotti, Jim, author.
Title: Joe Burrow vs. Dan Marino : who would win? / Jim Gigliotti.
Other titles: Joe Burrow versus Marino
Description: Minneapolis, MN : Lerner Publications, [2025] | Series: Lerner sports. All-star smackdown | Includes bibliographical references and index. | Audience: Ages 7–11 | Audience: Grades 2–3 | Summary: "NFL quarterbacks Joe Burrow and Dan Marino are both known for their quick, accurate passes. But which football signal-caller is better? Reviewtheir stats and greatest moments and make your choice."—Provided by publisher.
Identifiers: LCCN 2023048498 (print) | LCCN 2023048499 (ebook) | ISBN 9798765625880 (library binding) | ISBN 9798765628126 (paperback) | ISBN 9798765632123 (epub)
Subjects: LCSH: Burrow, Joe, 1996-—Juvenile literature. | Marino, Dan, 1961-—Juvenile literature. | Quarterbacks (Football)—United States—Biography—Juvenile literature.
Classification: LCC GV939.B873 G54 2025 (print) | LCC GV939.B873 (ebook) | DDC 796.332092 [B]—dc23/eng/20231101

LC record available at https://lccn.loc.gov/2023048498
LC ebook record available at https://lccn.loc.gov/2023048499

Manufactured in the United States of America
1 – CG – 7/15/24

TABLE OF CONTENTS

Dan Marino

INTRODUCTION

TWO STAR QUARTERBACKS

Dan Marino and Joe Burrow were born to play football. Marino grew up in an area that has produced many great quarterbacks in the National Football League (NFL). He became one of the

» Fast Facts «

- ✪ Dan Marino had his best season in 1984 with a record 5,084 passing yards and 48 touchdown passes.

- ✪ Marino led the Miami Dolphins to the 1984 conference championship.

- ✪ Joe Burrow led Louisiana State University to the 2019 national college championship.

- ✪ Burrow led the Cincinnati Bengals to the 2021 conference championship.

greatest quarterbacks in football history. Burrow went to high school not far from where the NFL began. He became a superstar NFL player in 2020.

Dan Marino's arm strength was legendary. It seemed as if he could throw a football through a brick wall. He also released the ball very quickly. The ball was out of his hand as soon as Marino decided where to throw it. No one in NFL history was faster at releasing the ball.

His arm was so strong and his release was so quick that Marino could make throws no one else could. From 1983 to 1999, he was one of the best quarterbacks in the NFL. He made the Pro Bowl nine times.

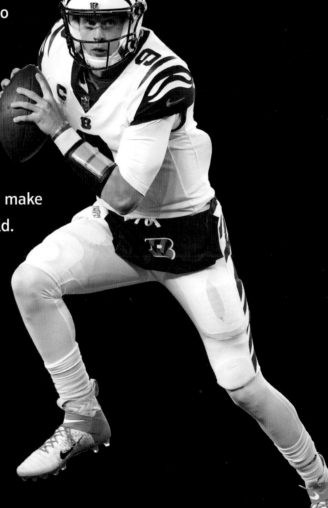

Joe Burrow

Joe Burrow's arm is not as strong as Marino's was. Burrow does not release the football as quickly as Marino did. But Burrow has other strengths. He has great agility. He can make plays by running the ball or throwing it.

Like Marino, Burrow is a very smart player. Burrow always seems to know the best place to throw the ball. His team knows it always has a chance to win when he is at quarterback. Marino's teammates felt the same way. But which player is better? That's up to you to decide. Let the smackdown begin!

Marino led the NFL in passing yards five times in his 17-year career.

In 2021, Burrow led the NFL by completing more than 70 percent of his passes.

CHAPTER 1

Marino throws a baseball in this photo from 1981.

GETTING STARTED

Dan Marino was born on September 15, 1961, in Pittsburgh, a city in western Pennsylvania. Johnny Unitas, Joe Namath, and George Blanda also grew up in that area. Joe Montana and Jim Kelly grew up near Pittsburgh at about the same time Marino did. All of them were NFL quarterbacks and are in the Pro Football Hall of Fame.

Marino was a football star in high school. But he also was a great baseball player. Marino was only 17 when the Kansas

City Royals selected him in the fourth round of the Major League Baseball Draft in 1979.

Marino chose football over baseball. Many colleges wanted Marino to play for their football teams, but he decided to stay close to home. He went to the University of Pittsburgh.

Marino had a great career at the school. He started at quarterback for four years. He helped the team win many games. But the 1983 NFL Draft was disappointing for him. Teams chose 26 other players before the Miami Dolphins selected Marino. Five teams took other quarterbacks instead of Marino. Finally, the Dolphins picked Marino with the 27th overall pick.

In four seasons at Pittsburgh, Marino had 79 touchdown passes.

Marino wanted to show the teams that had passed on him that they had made a mistake. He succeeded almost from the start. He wowed the Dolphins wide receivers with amazing throws in practice. He impressed the team's coaches with how smart he was. He made passes that no other quarterback on the roster could make.

Marino became the starting quarterback by the sixth game of his rookie season. He helped the Dolphins reach the playoffs and made the Pro Bowl. Most players don't reach the Pro Bowl in their first season.

Marino was the Miami starting quarterback from 1983 to 1999.

Marino gets ready to pass in a 1983 game.

Burrow (center) helped Athens High School reach the 2014 Ohio state playoffs.

Joe Burrow was born on December 10, 1996, in Ames, Iowa. His dad was a football coach. Burrow and his family moved often. His dad coached at different schools, and the family moved with him.

In Ohio, Burrow was a star player in high school. He won the Mr. Football Award as the best player in the state. Then he went to Ohio State University. He didn't play much there, but he graduated in only three years. That meant he could still play one more season of college football.

Burrow left Ohio State to attend Louisiana State University. He led the football team to the national championship. Burrow earned a master's degree in December 2019. He also won the 2019 Heisman Trophy as the best player in college football.

Burrow holds the national championship trophy after he threw five touchdown passes in the game. Louisiana State beat the Clemson Tigers 42–25.

Burrow led the Bengals against the Los Angeles Rams in the 2022 Super Bowl.

The Cincinnati Bengals took Burrow with the number one overall pick of the 2020 NFL Draft. It had been a long time since the Bengals had a winning team. Their fans hoped Burrow would turn the team around.

He was Cincinnati's starter right away. In his rookie season, the team won only four games. The next year, the Bengals were the surprise team of the NFL. They made it to the 2022 Super Bowl. The Bengals lost to the Los Angeles Rams 23–20.

CONSIDER THIS

The 1983 and 2020 NFL Drafts were among the best ever for quarterbacks. In 1983, Dan Marino was the last of six quarterbacks taken in the first round. In 2020, Joe Burrow was the first of three star passers among the first six picks.

Burrow makes good decisions when he chooses where to throw the ball.

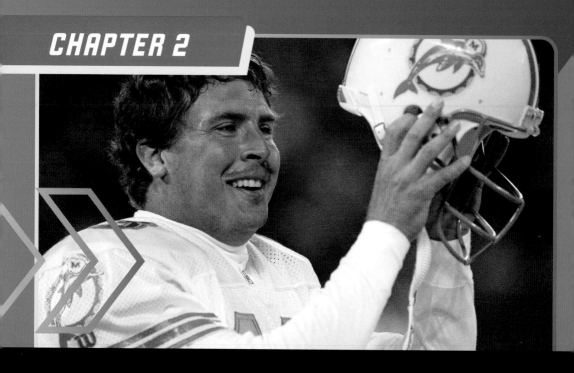

CHAPTER 2

GREATEST MOMENTS

In a 1994 game, the New York Jets led the Dolphins 24–21. The Dolphins had the ball near the end of the game. They drove from their 16-yard line to New York's 8-yard line. All of the yards came on passes by Marino.

With time running low, Marino signaled to his teammates that he was going to spike the ball into the ground. It would be an incomplete pass, but the game clock would stop running.

Marino was only pretending. Instead of spiking the ball, he threw a pass to Mark Ingram. The Jets were fooled. Ingram scored a touchdown! The Dolphins won 28–24.

Dan Marino could do many things very well. But what he did best was rally his team to win. During Marino's career, the Dolphins pulled off 36 wins in games they'd been losing in the fourth quarter.

In the 1984 American Football Conference Championship Game, Marino threw for 423 passing yards and four touchdowns. The Dolphins beat the Pittsburgh Steelers 45–28. That sent Marino and Miami to the Super Bowl. They lost that game to the San Francisco 49ers 38–16.

Marino (left) threw for 318 yards and a touchdown in his only Super Bowl appearance in 1985.

Burrow threw four touchdown passes in this 2021 win over the Ravens.

In 2020, Joe Burrow's rookie season ended after only 10 games. He hurt his knee and needed surgery. He returned to the field for the 2021 season. Though he was coming back from a terrible injury, Burrow thrilled fans with some of his greatest moments.

In Week 16, the Bengals blew out the Baltimore Ravens 41–21. Burrow set a Bengals record by passing for 525 yards. Only three NFL quarterbacks have had more yards in a game.

The next week, the Bengals trailed the Kansas City Chiefs in the fourth quarter. Burrow threw a touchdown pass. Then he threw two long passes to Ja'Marr Chase to set up the winning field goal. The Bengals were division champions.

Burrow was terrific in the 2021 playoffs. He led the team to three close wins. The third win came against the Chiefs. The game was tied in overtime. Burrow completed two passes to move the ball close enough for the winning field goal. The Bengals were conference champions. They had not won their conference since 1988!

Burrow gained 517 rushing yards in his first three NFL seasons.

CONSIDER THIS

Dan Marino and Joe Burrow both led their teams to the Super Bowl in their second seasons. They both lost the big game. Marino never made it back to the Super Bowl, though he came very close in 1992.

CHAPTER 3

After setting a new all-time passing yards record, Marino waved to cheering fans.

RECORD-SETTING SEASONS

Dan Marino was just getting warmed up during his great rookie season. The next year he became a superstar. In 1984, Marino passed for 5,084 yards. He was the first player in NFL history to top 5,000 yards in a season. No one would do it again until 2008.

Marino went on to lead the NFL in passing yards again in 1985, 1986, 1988, and 1992. In 1995, he broke the NFL record for career passing yards. He became the first player to pass for 50,000 yards in his career. Then he became the first to pass for 60,000 yards.

Of course, racking up passing yards is less important than scoring points and winning games. In 1984, he set another league record by throwing 48 touchdown passes. That mark stood for 20 years!

Marino again led the league in scoring tosses in 1985 and 1986. In 1995, Marino threw the 343rd touchdown pass of his career. That made him the NFL's all-time leader in passing touchdowns. He held this record until 2007.

Marino (center) celebrates with teammates after another scoring play.

Joe Burrow can light up the scoreboard almost as fast as Marino could. Burrow passed for 34 touchdowns in 2021. That was the most by any player in Bengals history. He passed for 35 scores in 2022 to break his own record. More importantly, he led his team to the playoffs both years. Burrow already has thrown for more yards in the playoffs than any other player in Bengals history.

Burrow is at his best in playoff games.

CONSIDER THIS

Dan Marino averaged 253.6 passing yards and 1.7 touchdowns per game in his 242 career regular-season games. Joe Burrow has averaged 280.3 yards per game in his 42 regular-season games through 2022. He has averaged 1.9 touchdown passes.

Burrow set a Bengals record with 414 completed passes in 2022.

CHAPTER 4

Marino's quick throwing style helped him reach the Hall of Fame.

AND THE WINNER IS

So who wins this quarterback smackdown? A good argument can be made for either strong-armed thrower. Dan Marino and Joe Burrow both have a lot of passing yards and passing touchdowns. They both are great at leading their teams to big victories.

Marino was a better passer than Burrow is. But Burrow has more agility and excels at running with the ball. Both quarterbacks reached the Super Bowl once and lost.

Marino held or tied 30 NFL records when he retired. Burrow hasn't played long enough to do the same. But he is rewriting the Bengals record book every season. Of Marino's 33 comeback victories in the regular season, six came in his first three years. Burrow is matching that pace. He has had five comeback wins in his first three years.

It seems as if Burrow only needs time to match the stats that Marino put up during his long career. The young star gets closer and closer every time he takes the field.

Burrow has 10 rushing touchdowns. Marino only had nine in 17 seasons.

Burrow calls a play.

Only a handful of quarterbacks in NFL history can match Marino's stats. Marino and the NFL's other great retired quarterbacks are in the Pro Football Hall of Fame. The way Burrow is going, he might join them there one day.

The winner of this smackdown is Marino! But you might have a different opinion. Who do you think the winner is? Consider their stories, then make your choice!

In 2003, the Dolphins retired Marino's jersey number. In his honor, no Dolphins player will wear number 13 again.

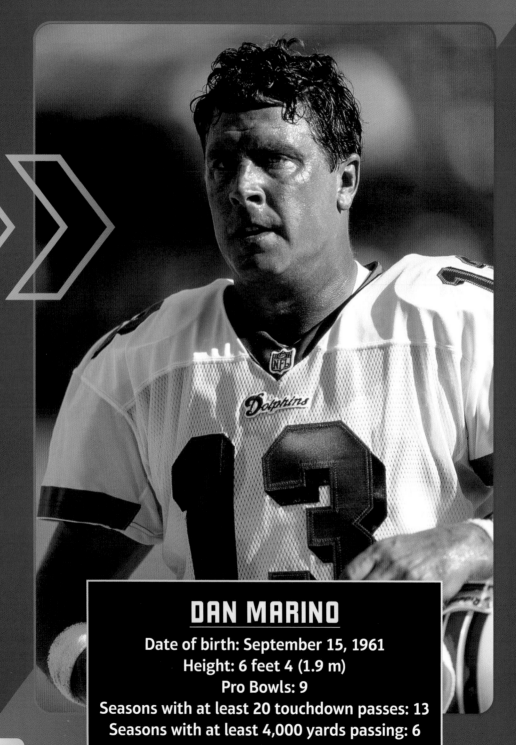

DAN MARINO

Date of birth: September 15, 1961
Height: 6 feet 4 (1.9 m)
Pro Bowls: 9
Seasons with at least 20 touchdown passes: 13
Seasons with at least 4,000 yards passing: 6

JOE BURROW

Date of birth: December 10, 1996
Height: 6 feet 4 (1.9 m)
Pro Bowls: 1
Seasons with at least 20 touchdown passes: 2
Seasons with at least 4,000 yards passing: 2

GLOSSARY

agility: the ability to move easily and quickly

conference: one of two groups of teams in the NFL, the American Football Conference and the National Football Conference

draft: when teams take turns choosing new players

field goal: a score of three points in football made by kicking the ball over the crossbar

pro: short for *professional*, taking part in an activity to make money

Pro Bowl: the NFL's all-star game

rally: to come from behind with a late burst of scoring

regular season: when all of the teams in a league play one another to determine playoff teams

rookie: a first-year player

roster: a list of players on a team

spike: to pass the football into the ground to stop the clock

start: to be on the field at the beginning of a football game

wide receiver: a football player whose main job is to catch passes

LEARN MORE

Abdo, Kenny. *Cincinnati Bengals.* North Mankato, MN: Fly!, 2021.

Cincinnati Bengals
https://www.bengals.com

Coleman, Ted. *Miami Dolphins All-Time Greats.* Mendota Heights, MN: Press Box Books, 2022.

Miami Dolphins
www.miamidolphins.com

Fishman, Jon M. *Joe Burrow.* Minneapolis: Lerner Publications, 2022.

Sports Illustrated Kids: Football
https://www.sikids.com/football

INDEX

PHOTO ACKNOWLEDGMENTS